Pots and Planters

in a weekend

MILLENNIUM

Pots and Planters
in a weekend

Julie London

JOURNEY EDITIONS
Boston • Tokyo

Acknowledgments

Thanks to everyone who has worked on this book – a testament to team effort.

First published in the United States in 2000 by Journey Editions, an imprint of Periplus Editions (HK) Ltd, with editiorial offices at 153 Milk Street, Boston, Massachusetts 02109.

ISBN:1-58290-028-0

Distributed in the U.S. by
TUTTLE PUBLISHING
DISTRIBUTION CENTER
Airport Industrial Park
364 Innovation Drive
North Clarendon, VT 05759-9436
Tel: (800) 526-2778
Tel: (802) 773-8930

Printed in Hong Kong
First US edition
06 05 04 03 02 01 00
10 9 8 7 6 5 4 3 2 1

Contents

Introduction

Pots and containers are a good introduction to gardening. Even if you do not have much space or gardening knowledge to begin with, you can plant a terracotta pot with geraniums for some summer color; this is when the gardening bug tends to hit you. This book has been designed to enable you to create some original and exciting pots and planters for your home and garden. The projects are small scale by their nature, except the tree painted on a wall, but that can be scaled up or down to suit the area. All of them are suitable for your garden or balcony, and if you are limited for space these containers will be ideal.

We have included ideas that are unusual, such as the cut-down pipes in the patio, for example, and you can adapt these as you wish. You may decide to choose different shapes or heights and to plant them in a completely different way, but the basic concept should provide a solid guide. We have also included some traditional ideas such as the wooden window box which sits on the sill but could just as easily be adapted to be attached to wall brackets.

We know that you will feel inspired to try out ideas of your own. Some of the best results arise from mistakes, so do not be afraid to stray from the exact designs and experiment for yourself. We have often made suggestions on alternative materials to use or ways of varying the design.

Some of the ideas for decorating would be equally successful on an alternative project. The Recycled containers project uses colored line drawings for découpage; photographs from magazines or postcards would give a very different look and could also be used to decorate a traditional wooden window box that is going to be used indoors.

All the tools and materials used in this book are easily available, usually from DIY stores and garden centers. You can obtain the gold leaf for the papier-mâché window box through craft or art shops. For other projects you may need to rent equipment. Day rates vary depending on the size of machinery. Otherwise we suggest you borrow from friends if you do not have all the tools. Also many of these ideas can be made with materials you probably have anyway, such as newspapers, pieces of wood and left over paint.

Of course, not everything in this book has to have a plant in it; decorated plant pots make useful storage on a desk, for instance, as do tin cans. So when the summer is over you can bring them indoors and give them a new lease of life around the house.

We really like the idea of making something from nothing and believe in recycling. For instance, in the case of the Recycled containers project, lettuce is grown in an old lunch box that had lost its lid. This planter would enjoy pride of place on any kitchen windowsill. Where you can, try to use existing materials rather than

buying new ones and change the designs to suit your materials.

Not all these projects are meant to last for ever. The glass containers are really an exercise in decoration; they can be used for an arrangement for a special occasion or for storing collections. Many of us have jars with shells and pebbles around the house that we cannot bear to part with; as well as looking attractive they provide inspiration for further decorative projects.

Whatever you make and however you make it, enjoy doing it.

Julie London

Lavender window box

Everybody has room for a window box, whether inside or out. Keep to one type of planting and co-ordinate the color for a dramatic visual effect.

You do not require any complicated skills to make a basic window box, and even if you use quite rough wood it will look good if the proportions are right. The ends of this one have been angled slightly to make it look more elegant, which also gives more planting space inside.

The window box can be made from one plank of wood. The base is cut to fit but the sides use the depth of the plank of wood, so there is minimal cutting. The feet are made from the scraps, using a glass as a guide to cut the arch shapes.

As well as putting this box on a windowsill it could also be fixed to a wall on brackets, with or without feet. Another option is to make it from odd bits of driftwood, either stuck onto a frame or fixed together to make a complete box.

The decoration utilizes existing materials. These tiles were leftovers from a friend's bathroom, but perfectly fitted the feel we wanted to create; you could also try using shells or beads to embellish the box. Perhaps pieces of broken pots could also be used to give a mosaic effect.

You could try making a larger box to hold patio tomatoes or other container vegetables during the summer. Or use several to edge a path.

Planning your time

DAY ONE
AM: Buy your materials; construct the main pieces

PM: Make and attach legs; paint on color

DAY TWO
AM: Attach tiles and/or decoration

PM: Plant up box. Put in place and admire

Tools and materials

**8 ft x 6 in x ¾ in
(2.4 m x 15 cm x 2 cm) Softwood**

Wood glue

Brads or Finishing nails

Drill

Right angle

Jigsaw

Pencil

Paintbrush

Hammer

Woodstain or paint

Tiles for decoration

1

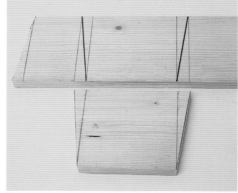

2

3

4

Day One

Step 1

Cut two pieces of wood 24 in (60 cm) long for the sides of the window box; and one piece 22 in (56 cm) for the base – which is less two thicknesses of the wood.

To make the end pieces, use the width of the wood to measure and mark across an offcut, using a right angle to make sure it is square.

Step 2

The ends need to be wider at the top than at the bottom to give a neat angle to the box. Measure ¾ in (2 cm) either side of the two lines you have drawn and mark a cutting line diagonally in between each set of lines.

Step 3

Join one side to one end with weatherproof wood glue. Then fix with brads or finishing nails.

Step 4

Join the base to the side and end with glue and brads or finishing nails. Join the other side in the same way.

Step 5

Before attaching the last end use it as a template to make the feet. Measure and divide the wood in half along the grain, and draw around the end to ensure it will fit the base of the window box.

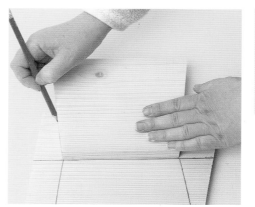

5

Using latex paint

If you are using up leftover latex paint to decorate your window box give it several coats of varnish to protect it from the elements.

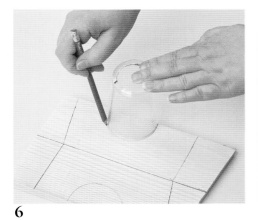

6

7

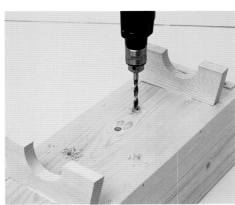

8

9

Step 6

Use a drinking glass as a guide to mark the arch shapes. Cut away the wood using a jigsaw.

Step 7

Mark the position of the feet, drill two holes through the base of the box for each foot and glue in place. Turn the box right side up and screw through the two holes for a secure fixture.

Step 8

Drill drainage holes through the base of the box.

Step 9

Paint on the woodstain, making sure you paint the underneath to protect the wood.

Day Two

Step 10

Fix on tiles for decoration using strong glue. Make sure the tiles are evenly spaced for an attractive design.

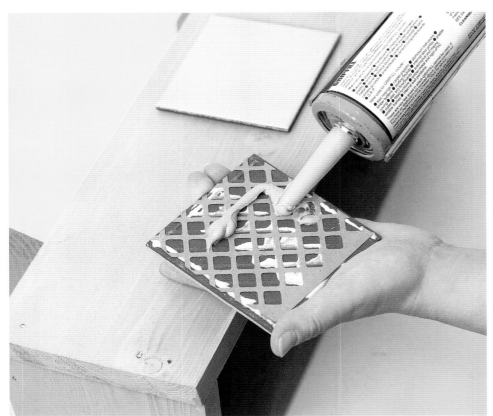

10

Silver ball planters on chains

Here is a fun idea for a focal point in the garden. These silver ball planters look great hung against a wall or from a tree, especially for a summer garden party.

Planning your time

DAY ONE
AM: Buy your materials and get chain cut to length at place of purchase

PM: Hollow out balls; attach hooks; spray paint

DAY TWO
AM: Plant suitable annuals, or if in winter months, plant ivies

PM: Position in garden, and enjoy

Tools and materials

3 foam children's soccer balls
3 galvanized S hooks
3 lengths of chain cut to size
Silver acrylic spray paint
3 suitable plants
Marker pen
Long-bladed scissors

This idea was inspired by the owner of a garden who had used cannonballs as hanging planters. As cannonballs are not readily available, however, we thought we should find something a little more accessible.

Foam soccer balls seemed to be an ideal solution; they are easy to find and not very expensive to buy. The trick is to hollow out the ball sufficiently to put in a plant and some potting soil with room for the plant to grow properly. You need to be careful that you do not make the sides of the ball too thin in case it starts to collapse. Also make sure that you insert the S hook well into the depth of the ball or it will pull the planter up into a point when it is full.

These balls were sprayed with silver acrylic paint, which seemed to cover them well. You also get a fantastic range of colors in spray paints. Enamel and latex paint do not work very well.

It is not a good idea to leave these planters out in cold or bad weather. If you plant them with Pearlwort (*Sagina subulata*), which has compact growth, you will need simply to mist them regularly with a water spray.

1

2

3

Day One

Step 1

Take one of the plants out of its pot and use the top of the pot to draw a circle on the surface of the balls. Use the biggest circumference of pot that you have.

Step 2

Cut around the marked circle with long-bladed scissors. You need to cut deep into the middle of the ball and remove the bits you have cut.

Step 3

Pull out more of the middle of the ball with your hand so that there is a decent-sized well in which the plant will have room to grow.

Step 4

Using one blade of the scissors, dig deep into the ball about 1 in (2.5 cm) back from the circular hole you have cut. Work the blade back up, to the side of the point of entry, onto the outside of the ball again to create a second small hole. Make sure you do not cut up through the surface of the ball.

4

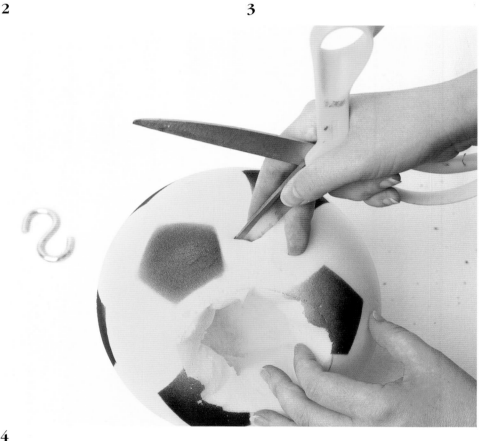

Colorful planting

You could plant these balls with seasonal plants such as trailing geraniums or petunias. A row of balls can create a visual division in the garden.

5

6

7

Step 5

Press the S hook into the first hole made with the scissors blade and work it up through the channel and out through the second hole.

Step 6

Hang the ball from the chain using the S hook. Then wrap the chain around a clothes line outside, or hang from a nail in a garage, and spray all over with silver acrylic paint. You will need to apply several coats. Remember to spray around the inside edge of the hole you have made in the ball, just in case the plant does not cover it completely.

Day Two

Step 7

Once the ball is dry, take it down and place it on a plant pot to keep it stable. Fill the hole with potting soil and put in the plant. Attach all the balls to their chains and hang in the garden or conservatory, and enjoy!

Square planter on platform with casters

This is a simple idea that allows you to move large plants around easily. You can steer them towards the light and save pulling your back muscles while you do so.

You often see plant platforms like this in magazine articles featuring smart Parisian apartments where the balconies overlook fantastic Art Nouveau buildings, but it is such a practical idea that there is no reason why it cannot be adopted in the smallest studio apartment.

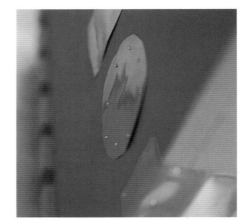

No doubt you have visited homes where a huge plant is stuck in the corner of the room because it is too big to move, with accumulating dust and piles of dead leaves that cannot be reached. Whether you keep plants in a conservatory or in a small flat this platform on casters will make life much easier for you.

The outer box is a decorative idea to hide an ugly plastic pot. Painted in contrasting colors, with tin decoration, it draws loose inspiration from the Mexican craft of making artifacts from discarded drink cans. The cans are cut with multi-purpose scissors that will cut anything. The copper panel pins add further decoration as well as hold the shapes in place. If you have children, however, it might be best to decorate the box with stencils to avoid the danger of little fingers being cut by sharp edges.

You could make the platform on its own and instead of making the box to cover the plant pot, spray the pot with an acrylic or enamel paint to create different effects, as in the Recycled containers project on page 70.

Planning your time

DAY ONE
AM: Buy your materials
PM: Cut out and assemble platform

DAY TWO
AM: Cut out and assemble box
PM: Paint and decorate with motifs

Tools and materials

24 ft x 1 in x 2 in
(7.5 m x 2.5 cm x 5 cm)
planed softwood

8 x 4 ft (2.5 x 1.2 m) sheet of
½ in (15 mm) plywood

Saw

Sandpaper

Multi-purpose scissors

No 8 woodscrews

PVA wood glue

2 magnetic catches

Several empty drink cans

Copper finishing nails

4 casters

Pencil

Screwdriver

Drill with countersink bit

Paint

1

Day One

Step 1

To make the base of the planter, cut eleven pieces of 1 x 2 in (2.5 x 5 cm) softwood battens to 20 in (50 cm) each.

Step 2

Lay eight of the battens out on the floor evenly spaced, using the narrow side of one as a spacer.

Step 3

Lay the batten you have just used as a spacer across the other battens and mark the central position where it crosses each one.

Careful measuring

Of course you can make the platform to fit the size of pot you have. Make sure you measure your pot carefully first to allow enough base for it.

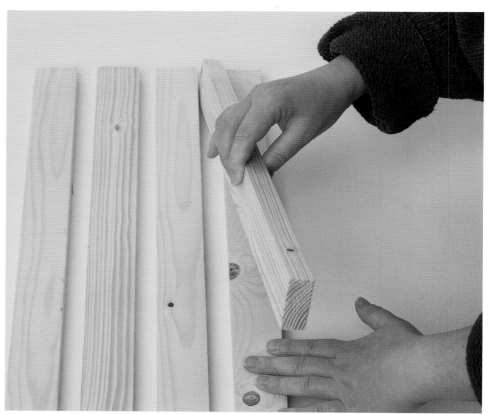

2

3

4

Step 4

Drill pilot holes and screw to each batten individually. Repeat this with the two other battens, putting one in the middle and one at the other end, measuring the same distance in from the edge as the first.

Step 5

Screw a caster to each corner, in between the first two screw heads, to complete the platform.

Day Two

Step 6

Cut four pieces of plywood, two 18 x 18 in (45 x 45 cm), and two 18 x 17½ in (45 x 43.5 cm). On one of the larger pieces mark the depth of the plywood against two opposite edges with a pencil. Drill three pilot holes as shown.

Step 7

Turn the square of plywood over and use the countersink tool on each hole so that the screw will sit level with the surface of the wood when it is screwed in.

5

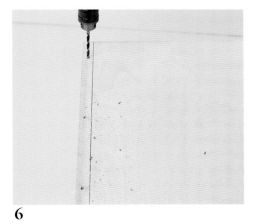

6

7

Using acrylic paint

You could try using an acrylic spray paint instead of latex to save the trouble of varnishing.

Step 8

Assemble three sides of the box, screwing through the holes you have made. To brace the inside of the box, cut two right-angled triangles from scraps of plywood. Mark their position on the inside of the box; there should be one in each corner. Drill holes through the box where you have marked. Countersink the hole on the outside of the box, and screw through the outside to secure the braces.

Step 9

To make the lip, cut four pieces of softwood to 20 in (50 cm) each. You need to mitre two of the corners. Fold a piece of paper to get a 45-degree angle, marking it on the batten as shown. Cut with a jigsaw or hand saw.

Step 10

Glue and pin the first lip in place, butting the second up to the first and the third to the second. Sand off any excess wood to make them fit. Fill any gaps and fill in the screw holes with wood filler. Sand off when the filler is completely dry.

Step 11

Mark the width of the plywood on each side of the remaining square that you cut earlier. There is no need to miter the last batten as it sits at right angles to the others. Screw the base plate of a magnetic catch just inside the marked line on each side of the square.

Step 12

Screw the top parts of the catches to the box. Attach them to their partners, and put the last side of the box in place. Mark the positions of the catches on the side of the box through the screw holes; disassemble and screw in place.

8

9

10

11

12

13

Step 13

Paint the box in contrasting colors and then varnish. Cut up drink cans for decoration using multi-purpose scissors.

Step 14

Flatten the tin by rolling it against its curl. Scratch shapes – a square and a circle – or draw around an appropriate object and cut out.

Step 15

Secure the shapes in place with copper finishing nails, which also look decorative.

Découpage decoration

An alternative to using tin decoration could be to découpage the box, cutting up pictures from magazines to complement the plant inside and pasting them on.

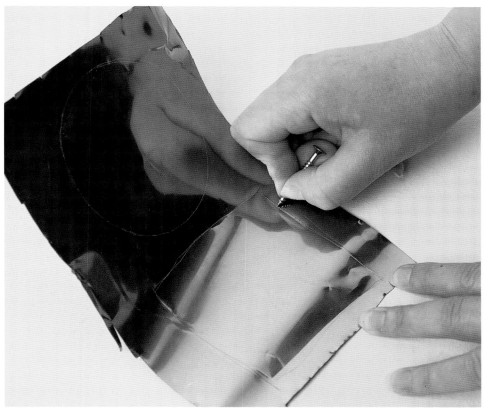

14

15

Hanging pots

Colorful hanging pots are ideal for keeping plants off the ground, especially for trailing plants such as strawberries, which tend to get eaten by slugs and snails.

This idea could be used as an alternative to a hanging basket, perhaps planted out with different bedding plants to match the colors of the pots. It looks best with trailing plants, such as petunias and geraniums, or plants with many branching stems, such as verbena, so that the color of the pot can be seen through the foliage.

The idea is probably most suited to strawberries. It is not dissimilar to the idea of a strawberry pot, which has different holes for individual plants. As the strawberries produce trailers, propagate them by rooting them into the empty pots.

All the pots and the pole from which they hang are painted with latex paint and will need to be recoated in subsequent years.

Another use for this project could be to hang the pole in a garden shed and to use the pots for storing twine, plant labels, seed packets and other such items. Instead of using terracotta pots you can spray ordinary plastic ones with acrylic paint and hammer them in place.

Planning your time

DAY ONE
AM: Buy your materials
PM: Cut pole; paint pots
DAY TWO
AM: Plant strawberries
PM: Hang in position

Tools and materials

Rustic stake

Copper common nails

Galvanized chain

Galvanized S hook to fit the chain

Nine terracotta plant pots with rims

Assorted paint colors

$\frac{1}{12}$ in (2 mm) galvanized wire

Jigsaw

Drill

Screw eye

Strawberry plants

Vice

Hammer

Pencil

Paintbrush

Paint

Day One

Step 1
Decide how long you want the pole to be, by seeing how many pots will look right along the length of it. Mark their positions with a pencil.

Step 2
Secure the pole in a vice, then cut it with a jigsaw.

Step 3
Drill a hole in one end of the pole for the screw eye.

Step 4
Use a screwdriver, spoon or stick as leverage to screw in the eye.

Step 5
Hammer in the copper nails at intervals along the pole to correspond with the number of pots, using the marks you have made as a guide.

Deciding on the length of the pole

You can make the pole as long as you like, depending on the number of pots you want to use.

1

2

3

4

5

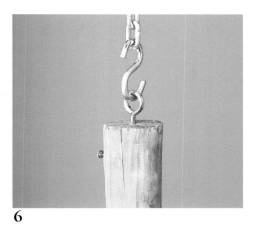

6

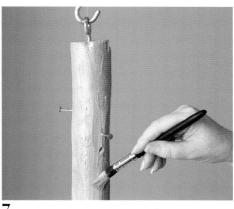

7

8

9

10

Step 6

Hang the pole on an S hook and chain and secure it around a clothes line, or even in its final position if it is accessible.

Step 7

Paint the pole in one of the colors you have chosen.

Step 8

Paint all the pots in a selection of colors to match and complement the pole.

Step 9

Cut a length of galvanized wire to fit one of the pots and twist it around itself so that it fits under the rim. Make a loop with the ends and hang it on one of the nails. Make any adjustments to the wire if necessary so that the pot is held securely.

Day Two

Step 10

Plant the strawberry plants. Leave some pots with just potting soil so that you can propagate the trailers later. Hang all the pots on the pole in a sheltered, sunny spot. Dib in the trailers as they grow to give you more plants.

Pipework patio

Break up the monotony of a paved patio by removing one or two slabs. Replace them with shaped pipework and cobbles to create a fragrant herb garden.

Planning your time

DAY ONE
AM: Buy your materials; hire the angle grind

PM: Lever up the slab and cut the pipes

DAY TWO
AM: Lay the pipes, pebbles and gravel

PM: Plant with low-growing herbs

Tools and materials

Paved patio

Tape measure

Felt-tip pen

Spade

Builders' sand

Potting soil

Terracotta rectangular pipe

Terracotta round pipe

Angle grind with masonry discs

Bag of large pebbles

½ in (10 mm) gravel

Length of wood

Hammer

Low-growing plants

This project uses the variety of shapes of ordinary drainage pipes. Each group of plants is contained within slices of pipe, levelled with the patio so that no one is likely to trip over them. The plants are scented, mainly thymes and chamomile, so if they are trodden on, which they probably will be, there will be a lovely aroma.

The round and oblong pipe used here came from a lumber yard, but you might pick up something similar at a garage sale. You will need an angle grind to cut the pipe. These can be rented for a day unless you know someone who can lend one to you. You will need 3–5 cutting discs depending on how many pipes you intend to cut and how thick they are. One of the pipes that we thought was terracotta was in fact concrete "in terracotta clothing" and took a lot more cutting than we had anticipated. So be prepared.

Another idea would be to leave the pipes taller and plant them at the edge of a patio, all at different heights. They should be embedded into the earth firmly. Or you could cast shapes such as seashells from concrete and plant around the outside. Try sowing annuals for summer color or plant low-growing spring bulbs.

Day One

Step 1

Decide where you want to locate the planted area in your patio. Ease the paving slab up with a spade, or crowbar, and remove it. You will need some help with this as paving slabs are extremely heavy.

Step 2

Measure the depth of the paving slab; this will ensure that you cut the pipes to the same depth as the paving stone.

Step 3

Transfer this measurement to the terracotta pipes and mark with a felt pen all the way round each pipe.

Step 4

Cut around each pipe with an angle grind. Make as many shapes as you need to fit the space.

Step 5

Add more sand to the area to bed the cut pipes into. Spread the sand evenly.

1

2

3

4

5

6

7

8

Day Two

Step 6
Arrange the pipe shapes and embed them into the sand.

Step 7
Fill in the gaps between the pipes with large pebbles.

Step 8
Make sure the pebbles and pipes are the same level as the patio. Use a length of wood to span the area, resting on the slabs either side. Tamp down with a hammer or mallet until the pipes and pebbles are even.

Step 9
Fill around the pebbles with gravel.

Step 10
Fill the cut pipes with potting soil, or earth from other parts of the garden, and plant with low-growing herbs.

Making the patio permanent

If you wanted to cement pipes and pebbles in place, brush cement in between the gaps, as you would when laying a patio. Wet the cement and leave to dry. Do this before you add plants to the containers.

9

10

Mirrored sconce

This mirrored sconce idea was inspired by the mirrored backs you sometimes see on wall-mounted candle holders which help to reflect light around a room.

Planning your time

DAY ONE
AM: Buy your materials; cut out shape

PM: Stick on pieces of mirror and leave to dry overnight

DAY TWO
AM: Grout and leave to dry; spray pot

PM: Attach to a wall

Tools and materials

Scrap of medium density fiberboard (MDF), or plywood

2–3 mirrored tiles

Waterproof tile and grout

Jigsaw with scrolling action

Packet of mirrored circles

Store-bought plant holder

Drill with masonry drill bit

Coach bolt

Acrylic spray paint

Filling knife

Sandpaper

These fragments of mirror are an attractive feature in a small garden, helping to promote the feeling of space and make the garden look bigger. Once you have mastered making this you could make a much larger one to hang as a piece of art on a garden wall or fence. You could also mosaic a window box with mirror pieces.

Be careful when breaking mirror tiles as the shards will cut; it is sensible to wear a pair of gardening gloves. Wrap up well in newspaper the pieces you are not going to use and throw them away safely.

The pot holder used here is a store-bought one, but another way of suspending the pot would be to attach the sconce to the wall with a large hook through the hole drilled in the center; a pot could be hung from this using a length of galvanized wire.

The silver plant pot is the original black plastic one that the geranium came in, simply sprayed with acrylic silver paint – which just goes to show that you make the most mundane object look special with a lick of paint.

You could try positioning several of these mirrored sconces to reflect the sun at different times of the day, especially if you have a shady garden. Or make a large one as a feature or focal point at the end of a path.

1

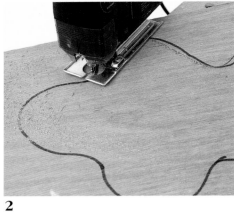

2

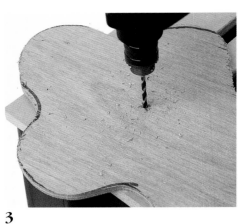

3

Day One

Step 1
Draw the shape of the sconce on a scrap of wood; plywood is used here.

Step 2
Cut the shape out with a jigsaw using the scrolling action.

Step 3
Drill a hole in the center of the shape for fixing later.

Step 4
Sand off the edges of the wood with sandpaper around a cork block, or wrap the sandpaper around a box of matches.

Step 5
Wrap the mirror tiles up in leftover wallpaper, or newspaper, and smash them with a hammer.

Step 6
You should now have many fragments of mirror. Carefully discard any really small shards.

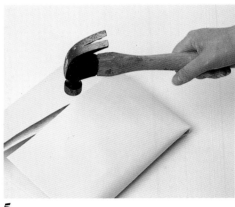

4

5

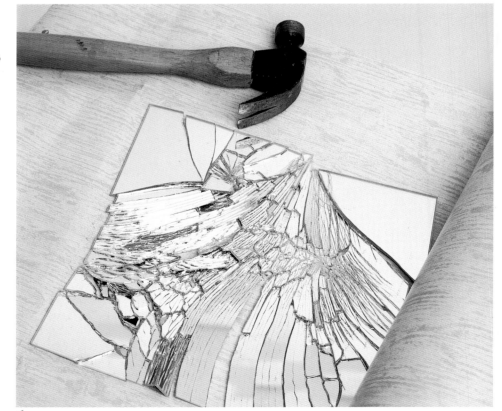

6

7

8

9

10

Step 7
Roughly arrange the pieces of mirror fragments and bought mirrored circles. Play around with the design before you commit yourself to sticking them down permanently.

Step 8
Apply a reasonably thick layer of adhesive to the wood with a filling knife.

Step 9
Arrange the pieces of mirror according to your design and leave to dry overnight.

Day Two

Step 10
Grout in between the pieces of mirror and wipe away the excess with a rag. Do not let too much grout dry on the mirrors as it will take you ages to scrape it off.

Step 11
Spray the flower pot with an acrylic spray paint. Fix the mirrored sconce to the wall using a coach bolt and washer and place the plant pot in the plant holder.

11

Fountain planter

The trickle of water in a garden must be on the top of everyone's list of favorite sounds and you do not need a huge garden for this unusual water feature.

Planning your time

DAY ONE
AM: Buy your materials

PM: Assemble the pump; pack with pebbles and sand

DAY TWO
AM: Fill with potting compost; dress with sand; plant Thrift; arrange pebbles and shells

PM: Switch on the pump, sit back and enjoy the sound of trickling water

Tools and materials

Large glazed pot

Smaller plastic plant pot

Small water pump fitted with a fountain attchment

Bag of large pebbles

Flexible tubing to fit the pump and equal to the circumference of the inner pot.

Bag of shells

Play sand

Thrift (*Armeria maritima*)

In fact, you do not even need a garden at all for this fountain planter as it will fit on a small balcony. This is a lovely project to make and will really fire your imagination. We have chosen to give the planter a seaside theme by the choice of plants and by using sand, pebbles and shells; of course you can make yours whatever you want.

This project involves more of an assembly of components than actually making something but, as the adage goes, the total is often more than the sum of the parts. Everything used here was bought at a garden center, but there is scope for you to use individual items, incorporate little sculptures, small boats, pieces of broken china or such.

Before assembling the project decide where you want to position it, because it will be impossible to move once it is full of sand, pebbles and water. The glazed pot is heavy enough when it is empty.

When assembling the pump* always follow the manufacturer's instructions and if needed, be sure to use an extension cord specifically designed for outdoor use. Remember also to bring the pump in during the winter months to protect it from frost should you live in a cold climate.

As an alternative indoor fountain try submerging the pump in a large glass tank or container and covering it with pebbles or shells.

note: The water pumps sold at most pond supply and garden centers may be too large for this project. For smaller water features contact The Fountain Company (800-955-7868; www.egglight.com).

Day One

Step 1

Decide the position of the fountain planter, and place the glazed pot on four large pebbles so that it is evenly balanced.

Step 2

Feed the plug-end of the pump cable through the drainage hole in the bottom of the large pot. If the hole is not large enough to slide the plug through, train the cable up the side of the pot and secure temporarily with masking tape.

Step 3

Place the pump in the small pot and put it roughly in the position you want it to be (centered vs. flush with the edge of the larger pot).

Step 4

Sit the small pot on a bed of sand, to raise its edge level with the edge of the outer pot.

Step 5

Half fill the small pot with large stones to keep the pump in place. Pack around the base of the planter with sand. You will not need a great depth of potting soil for the plants because Thrift has shallow roots. Continue filling with sand approximately ¾ up to the edge.

Hiding the pump cable

Position the planter so the electrical cable is to the back of the pot, camouflaged by foliage. Or use an arrangement of pebbles.

1

2

3

4

5

6

Step 6

Put a plastic bag over the pump and pebbles in the smaller pot to prevent soil getting into the container and clogging the pump when it is in action.

Day Two

Step 7

Fill up the large pot with potting soil to just below the rim.

Step 8

Plant Thrift around the edge of the glazed pot and top-dress with sand. Arrange shells in the sand; then fill the pump planter with pebbles shells and water.

Seaside theme planting

Other possible plants that might be suitable for growing in a seaside fountain include *Eryngium* (Sea Holly) and *Echinops ritro* (Veitch's Blue).

7

8

Papier-mâché window box

Transform a plastic window box by covering it in papier-mâché, string and gold leaf and bring a dash of glamor to a kitchen windowsill.

Planning your time

DAY ONE
AM: Buy your materials; apply first layer of paper

PM: Apply second, third and further layers of paper

DAY TWO
AM: Apply string decoration and further layers of paper

PM: Paint; apply gold leaf and varnish

Tools and materials

Plastic window box
Newspaper
PVA glue
Paint kettle
Paint
Paintbrushes
String
Gold leaf
Acrylic gold size
Spray varnish

This is really the art of camouflage – taking something mass produced and functional such as an ordinary green, white or terracotta plastic window box and turning it into an individual piece.

When applying the papier-mâché the layers of paper should run alternately for maximum strength – the first layer runs down the tray, the second across. Continue like this until there is enough. Each layer must dry before you apply the next one, so you may have to work out the timing carefully if you want to complete the window box by Sunday night. PVA glue is very strong once it is dry, so you may need fewer layers of paper than you think.

The string pattern trapped under a couple of layers of paper provides a relief to the sides of the trough that belies its humble origins; when highlighted with fake gold leaf it brings a touch of distinction. Fake gold leaf is available from craft shops and is extremely easy to use. Apply it on top of size, which is a glue substance, and then rub off the excess. You can be as rough as you like without causing any damage to it.

As this container is covered with paper it is not suitable for outdoor use or planting, but is appropriate for an indoor windowsill where the plants stay in their pots and are placed in the trough. However, as the inside is plastic you will be able to water them without any problems.

Day One

Step 1
Cover your work area with newspaper or wallpaper. Tear up several sheets of newspaper into roughly 2 in (5 cm) square pieces.

Step 2
Paste several pieces with PVA glue. The first layer needs to be stuck well to the plastic trough.

Step 3
Cover the plastic trough with torn pieces of paper. Make sure they are thoroughly stuck down. Leave to dry.

Step 4
Dilute the glue with water, adding about four parts water to one part glue, but you do not have to be too accurate about this. Soak some of the other pieces of paper in the solution. Cover the box again completely with paper and leave to dry.

Do this three or four more times, until there is a reasonable thickness of paper, leaving the paper to dry out between applications.

Day Two

Step 5
Cut some lengths of string to make a decoration and practice your pattern. Paste a thick line of glue along where you want to stick the string.

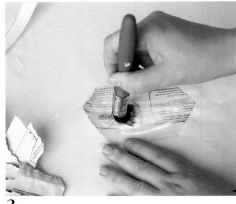

1

2

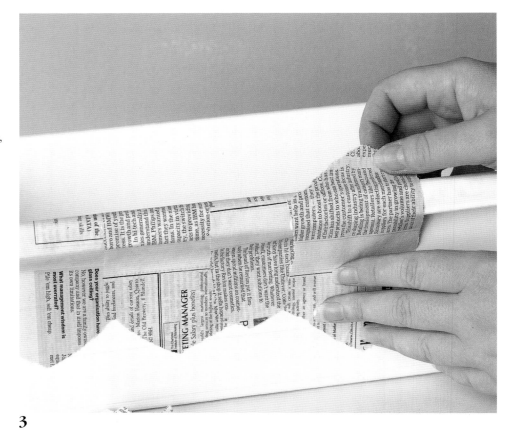

3

4

5

Step 6

Stick the string to the glue and hold in place. Follow the natural contours of the string, otherwise you will be fighting against it. Leave to dry.

Step 7

Tear up some more paper and soak the pieces in diluted glue. Cover the string with the paper, pressing it into the contours. Leave to dry.

Step 8

Continue to add glue-soaked paper to the surface until you achieve the desired effect. Leave to dry.

Step 9

Paint on two or three coats of acrylic paint. Leave to dry.

Step 10

Follow the relief lines of the string with acrylic gold size on a fine art brush. Leave until tacky, then apply the gold leaf to the size. Rub away the excess gold leaf with fingers and apply to other areas. Then, spray on a coat of acrylic varnish to protect the surface.

Varnishing papier-mâché

Use watered-down PVA glue as a sealant as an alternative to varnish.

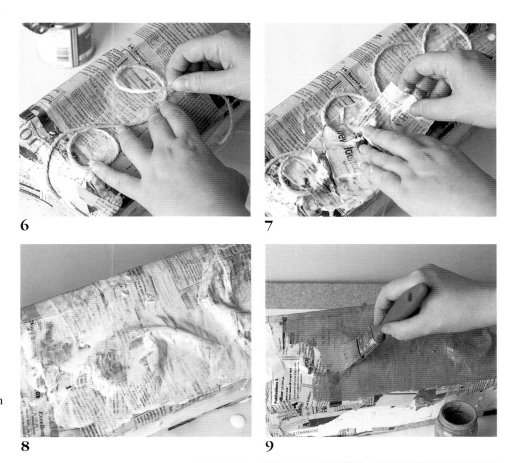

6

7

8

9

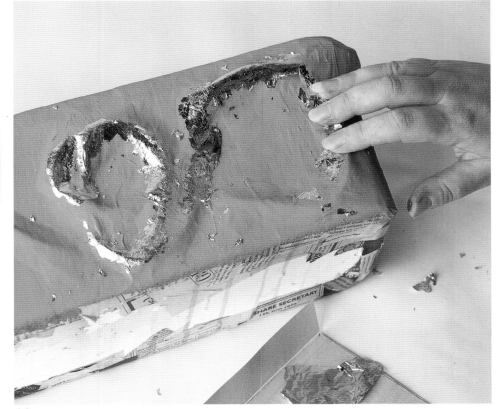

10

Sundial planter

A sundial is a whimsical piece of garden ornamentation, and this one with its twiggy gnomon—the arm that casts the shadow—and alpine plants is particularly unusual.

Planning your time

DAY ONE
AM: Buy your materials

PM: Paint pots; plant alpines; top dress with gravel

DAY TWO
AM: Make gnomon

PM: Set sundial at 12 noon

Tools and materials

Large bowl-shaped terracotta pot

Long tom style pot, the same height as the bowl pot

Paint

Potting soil

White gravel

Four small sedums or other alpines

Hazel or willow twigs

Elastic band

Jute

Weatherproof wood glue

This sundial is probably as accurate as most. The sun does the work of telling the time; all you have to do is to put the planter in the right position. The best way to do this is to set it by a watch; just move the container so that the gnomon casts the shadow at the time on the watch. The alpines represent the hour, quarter hours and half hour – 12, 3, 6, 9. So it is quite simple. Put the planter in a position where it is in full sun all day long. There is no point putting it in a part of the garden that is in shade for any length of time.

The sundial can be planted with any low-growing plants. Avoid using any plant that is likely to grow tall and cast its own shadow; these sedums are ideal because they hug the ground or gravel.

Another idea is to make a little knot garden with low-clipped boxwood; however, this would need a fair amount of maintenance to keep it in shape.

The gnomon is a bit arbitrary. We have found twigs that had a sort of fork in them that matched the 45-degree angle; you might have to hunt carefully before you find the right one. Or you could try asking an amenable florist for any suitable spare twigs. As an alternative to the twig, try twisting and bending a wire coat hanger into shape. A length of bamboo also makes an attractive arm for a sundial.

Day One

Step 1
Paint both pots with the same color paint. An off-white has been used to match the gravel.

Step 2
Put the smaller pot upside down in the middle of the larger one.

Step 3
Fill around the smaller pot with potting soil.

Step 4
Plant the four alpines at twelve, three, six and nine o'clock.

Step 5
Cover the soil with a layer of gravel, tucking it under and around the plants.

Evergreen planting

Choose evergreen plants that have form all year round, such as some of the miniature euphorbias, compact grasses and alpines.

1

2

3

4

5

6

7

8

9

10

Day Two

Step 6

To make the gnomon, make a 45-degree angle by folding a piece of paper. Find a corresponding angle on a long piece of hazel twig to cast the shadow. Cut a smaller piece of twig, about the same diameter of the upturned base of the smaller pot. Hold them together as near as you can using an rubber band.

Step 7

Cut another piece of twig and bind it with jute to the other pieces to make a right angle. Cover the rubber band with jute.

Step 8

Dab wood glue on the jute joints to stop the twigs slipping.

Step 9

Coat some of the gravel with glue at the points where the gnomon will be secured to the upturned pot. Try out the arrangement of gravel before you commit yourself to glue.

Step 10

Attach the gnomon to the glued gravel, making sure it is upright. Add more glue if it is a bit unsteady.

To set the sundial, choose which plant is to be twelve o'clock. Using an accurate watch, at midday put the sundial in position with the shadow directly in the middle of the plant.

Decorated plant pots

Plain unadorned plastic plant pots can be boring to look at. Decorate them to match your style, interior decoration or the colors of the plants they contain.

Planning your time

DAY ONE
AM: Buy plant pots and other materials

PM: Paint pots; decorate string and jute pots

DAY TWO

AM: Glue on nuggets, buttons, ribbon and shells

PM: Glue on buttons; spray shell pot; put plants in pots

Tools and materials

A selection of terracotta plant pots

Paint

Ribbon (wide and narrow)

Jute

Parcel string

Buttons

Shells

Spray paint

Hot melt glue gun

PVA glue

Glass nuggets

Paintbrush

Adhesive putty

Terracotta plant pots are very attractive but the plastic ones are lighter, cheaper and can be embellished and decorated in many different ways.

The possibilities are endless, but the best starting point is to consider the setting in which the pots will be placed. Use colors to match or contrast the room; the odd dregs of paint that are left over from decorating can be put to good use. Unusual decorative features can be created from quite ordinary items you have lying around  the house, such as buttons, ribbon, jute and string. Other ideas for decoration are to apply photocopies, pictures from magazines, or stamps. You could try sticking dried leaves or pressed flower heads on the pots and sealing them with varnish. Newsprint, the pages of an old encyclopedia, or wine labels could also look interesting. Special seasonal decorations are always an option, too. Take these ideas and adapt them to any size or shape of pot.

The only disconcerting thing about a plant pot is its shape; you should take the fact that it tapers into account when you plan your decoration. Have a practice first. Try the design out with adhesive putty before finally gluing three-dimensional decorations into place.

Plant pots can be put to other uses as well as for putting plants in. Use them for storing make-up, soaps or toothbrushes in a bathroom.

1

Day One

Step 1

You will need to paint the plant pots with a base color appropriate to the colors you are using for the string and ribbon pots as the pot will show through. Here cream and blue have been used.

Step 2

To attach string to the painted plant pot, cover the top 1 in (2.5 cm) with PVA glue. Let it go a bit tacky.

Step 3

Starting at the top, wind string around the pot. Follow the natural curl of the string or it may spring away from the pot. Continue until you reach the bottom, adding more glue as you go. Cut the end of the string off at an angle so that it fits neatly.

Cover the jute pot in the same way.

2

3

Day Two

Step 4
Try out the position of the nuggets using adhesive putty. When you are happy with the arrangement, stick them down permanently with a hot melt glue gun. Do a line at a time as you will have to hold the nuggets in place while the glue dries or they will slide off the surface of the pot.

Step 5
On a plain terracotta plant pot with a lip, glue or putty an odd assortment of buttons around the rim.

4

Appropriate decoration

Try to match the decoration of your plant pots to complement the plant or contents, such as choosing string to cover a pot that holds a cactus. Use a plant pot to store foreign loose change and bank notes and decorate the rim by gluing on foreign coins.

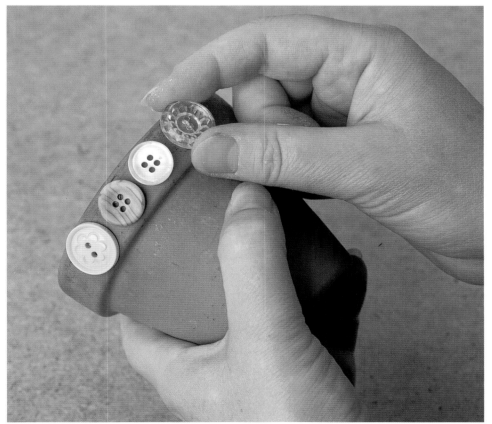

5

6

Step 6

To weave ribbon around a pot, first cut six equal lengths of wide ribbon enough to fold over the top and bottom of the pot.

Step 7

Stick the top of the ribbon inside the top edge of the pot. Glue the bottom under the pot.

Step 8

Weave the narrower ribbon under and over the wide strips you have just stuck down. Cut each piece as you use it and stick down under a piece of ribbon at the back of the pot.

7

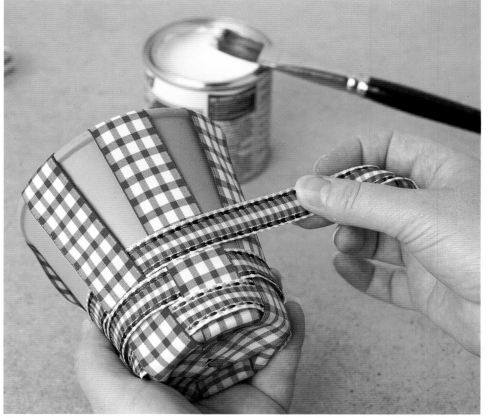

8

9

Step 9

For the shell pot, select the shells you want to use, and check how they will fit together using adhesive putty. Glue them onto the pot with a hot melt glue gun.

Step 10

Hold the shells in place while they dry.

Step 11

When you have finished sticking the shells on and the glue is dry, put the pot on a sheet of newspaper or wallpaper and spray with enamel paint.

10

Applying texture

Coat a plain pot in glue and roll it in sand for an all-over textured effect. Or apply the glue in stripes for alternating smooth and textured bands.

11

Painted tree planter

This painted tree on a brick wall is a simple idea that brings the effect of a colorful garden to a basement apartment or a pleasant view to an eyesore.

This stylized tree displays blossoms of trailing geraniums, but it can bear whatever type of flower you want it to. It will brighten any redundant area of your garden and is very easy to create.

There is a template for the tree at the back of the book, but if you are more confident at drawing freehand or want to discover a latent talent, get painting! Do not worry if you make a mistake; just incorporate it into your design or paint over it.

Make this tree whatever size you want, but check that it fits comfortably in the space you have allotted to it. Try curling it into and around corners of the building, over drainpipes. It could be used to disguise ugly downspouts if painted in the same color. The tree is a feature that you can keep adding to as the fancy takes you. You could hide a bird box in its branches and see who moves in.

The plants used here are continental trailing geraniums, which look lovely when in flower in the summer, but during the winter you could substitute ivies or other evergreen trailing plants.

Of course, if you have had enough of changing plants around you could always paint in your own permanent ones.

This project works especially well where there is not much opportunity for a garden, such as a basement area that has little space available for large plants.

Planning your time

DAY ONE
AM: Make template; transfer to wall

PM: Paint outlines; apply second and third colors

DAY TWO
AM: Paint pots; screw into masonry

PM: Plant up pots and hang in place

Tools and materials

A white-painted brick wall

Paint in three shades of the same color (blue)

Paintbrush

Terracotta pots

Screws

Masonry wall plugs

Drill

Screwdriver

$\frac{1}{16}$ in (1.5 mm) galvanized wire

Wallpaper or newspaper to make a template

Pencil or marker pen

1

Day One

Step 1

Roughly draw out your design on the reverse side of a piece of wallpaper. If you are using the templates on page 77 trace these and enlarge as necessary.

Step 2

When you are satisfied with your idea cover the proposed area with lengths of wallpaper. Join them together and attach them to the wall with masking tape.

Step 3

Transfer the bones of your design to the wallpaper freehand or using your tracings. Stand back every so often to make sure the tree looks alright from a distance.

2

3

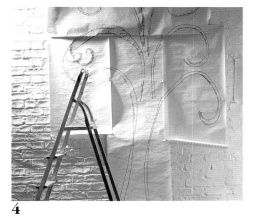

4

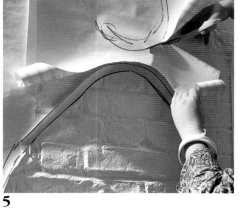

5

6

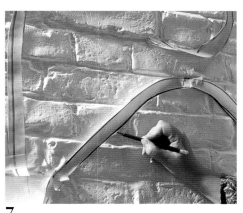

7

Step 4
The outlines of the branches of the tree as well as the trunk need to be reasonably thick so that there is some substance to the overall structure of the tree.

Step 5
Cut the tree out while it is still taped so that you do not lose the position. Restick it to the wall as you go along.

Step 6
You should now be left with the basic outline of the tree stuck to the wall.

Step 7
Draw around the cut-out pieces of wallpaper with a pencil and remove the paper as you go along.

Step 8
Paint in the outline you have just made with the deepest of the three paint tones you have chosen.

8

Don't be discouraged!

Painting on brick is harder than you think. You have to make several brush strokes to achieve an even effect.

9

Step 9

Using freehand brush strokes, add extra "branches" with the second color, to create more depth. Then add highlights with the third, lightest color.

Day Two

Step 10

Paint all the pots white, and leave to dry.

Step 11

Using a pencil, mark the positions of where the pots will hang on the tree. Drill pilot holes with a masonry drill bit, and plug with a hard wall plug. Finally attach a screw from which to hang the pot. Do this over all the branches of the tree for as many pots as necessary.

10

11

12

14

Step 12

Cut lengths of galvanized wire. Twist the wire under the lip of each pot, and make a loop by twisting the ends together. There is no particular way to do this; just make sure that the wire will support the pot on the wall.

Step 13

Plant up the pots with your choice of plants; trailing geraniums were used here.

Step 14

Hang each pot from its screw and stand back to enjoy.

13

Glass containers

Glass vases tend not to be very attractive when they are empty, so why not make something of them while they are waiting for those dozen red roses?

Planning your time
....
DAY ONE
AM: Buy/assemble your materials; cut bamboo canes

PM: Tie bamboo with jute; plant orchid

DAY TWO
AM: Assemble large container with sand, pebbles, shells

PM: Wash gravel; spray gravel; assemble gravel container

Tools and materials
....
Tall round glass container

Large square glass container

Small rectangular glass container

4 bamboo canes

Jute

Gravel

Acrylic spray paint

Play sand

Pebbles

Shells

Hacksaw

Tealights

Candles

Moth orchid

Pencil

E very time you visit the beach make a conscious effort to pick up shells and pebbles, bits of wood, glass nuggets rounded by the sea and various odd items, so that you can save them for exciting projects. Whenever you go to the sea put the day's "catch" in a glass jar and write the day and place on a piece of paper and put it in the jar as a reminder. This is what inspired this container project.

These are just a few ideas for a collection of glass containers that can be made up for a special occasion or to show off a collection of favorite objects.

Bamboo is used to hide the soil in which an orchid is planted; the orchid actually sits on top of the soil because it has air roots.

The gravel idea coordinates with the candles and keeps them firm near the top of the container so that the glass does not crack from the heat of the flames.

As a finishing touch a square vase with sand, pebbles and shells brings the atmosphere of the coast to any dining room.

These are ideas to decorate a table for a special occasion. At Christmas fill them with fairy lights or glittering baubles, with small wrapped presents for friends.

1

Day One

Step 1
Measure the bamboo against the inside of the tall round container and mark with a pencil.

Step 2
Cut the bamboo with a hacksaw.

Step 3
Cut more pieces of bamboo the same length; use the piece you have cut to measure against the rest of the canes. Cut as many pieces as necessary.

Joining bamboo
To join bamboo with jute try gluing it in place to make it easier to handle.

2

3

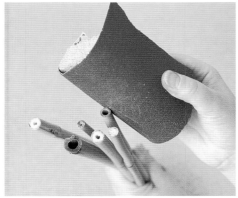

4

5

6

Step 4
Sand the edges of the pieces of bamboo smooth as it has a tendency to splinter.

Step 5
Lie the pieces of bamboo on a flat surface and tie them together with lengths of jute, looping around each one. Do this at the top and bottom.

Step 6
Put the tied pieces of bamboo in the container, spreading them around the inside. Then fill a third full with gravel for drainage.

Step 7
Top up with potting soil. Take care not to get any between the bamboo and the glass or the effect will be spoiled.

7

8

9

10

Step 8

Plant the orchid in the top of the soil.

Day Two

Step 9

To fill the large square container, put in play sand to about a third of the way up. Make sure it is dry, as it will not dry out when compacted in a container.

Step 10

Add a layer of white, and then black, pebbles.

Step 11

Top up with shells and wedge tealights in between the shells.

11

12

14

Step 12
To prepare the small rectangular container, wash the gravel to remove dirt and dust.

Step 13
Lay the gravel out on sheets of newspaper or wallpaper to dry thoroughly.

Step 14
Spray the gravel with an acrylic spray paint. Roll it around with the paper so that all sides are properly coated. You might need to do this in batches to get enough gravel to fill the container. Leave the gravel to dry completely, then fill the container and sit the candles in the top of the gravel.

13

Coloring gravel

Another way to color gravel is to put it in a plastic bag with spray paint and shake until it is completely covered. Then spread it out over paper to dry.

Oval planter

This plywood planter makes a stunning focal point in a contemporary living room, especially when holding a group of stylish plants such as these lilies.

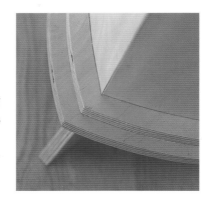

Birch plywood has such an attractive grain that it is a shame to cover it up with paint. A coat of varnish is all that is needed to bring the grain out and protect the surface.

The shape of this planter is reminiscent of a 1930s ocean liner with its pointed ends. As a shape it just evolved while we were making it, but the result is visually satisfying. All these materials are available from a lumber yard. However, if you cannot find 1/16 in (1.5 mm) veneer you can use 1/8 in (3 mm) instead, but it will be a bit harder to manipulate.

No special tools are required but you may need someone to help you, however, as getting the curve right is quite tricky on your own. The top and bottom frames are vital in keeping the curve of the sides, so it is important you get these bits right.

It is possible to make this planter any size you want it to be to suit the space you have available. Varnish the base well so that you ensure it is as waterproof as possible; it may be as well to put a plastic liner in the bottom if you have a tendency to overwater plants.

An alternative is to make the two edges of the planter, the base and the feet from medium density fiberboard and paint them. Leave the sides in birch plywood to make an attractive contrast.

Planning your time

DAY ONE
AM: Buy your materials; cut out two frames

PM: Cut out sides, base and feet and assemble

DAY TWO
AM: Attach base and sides; coat with varnish

PM: Apply second coat of varnish

Tools and materials

Jigsaw

⅜ in (10 mm) flat wood drill bit

Curve (plastic curtain track)

8 ft x 4 ft x ¾ in
(2.5 m x 1.2 m x 18 mm) birch or other plywood

8 ft x 4 ft x 1/16 in
(2.5 m x 1.2 m x 1.5 mm) birch or other veneer
(see box on page 68)

Marking gauge

Screws

Wood filler

Metal tape measure

Craft knife

Metal ruler

Screwdriver

Satin acrylic varnish

Paintbrush

Sandpaper

Wood glue

1

Day One

Step 1
Mark out a rectangle measuring 150 x 75 in (60 x 30 cm) on the sheet of ¾ in (18 mm) ply and divide it into four. To make the curve use a piece of flexible wood or plastic curtain track. Make sure it hits the intersections on one of the long halves of the rectangle. Ask someone to mark around the curve while you hold it.

Step 2
Repeat on the other side to make an ellipse shape.

Step 3
With a flat wood drill bit, drill a pilot hole near to the curved line just drawn. The hole should be big enough to insert the jigsaw blade. Cut along the line of the ellipse. Ask your helper to support the center while you cut as the wood will be heavy.

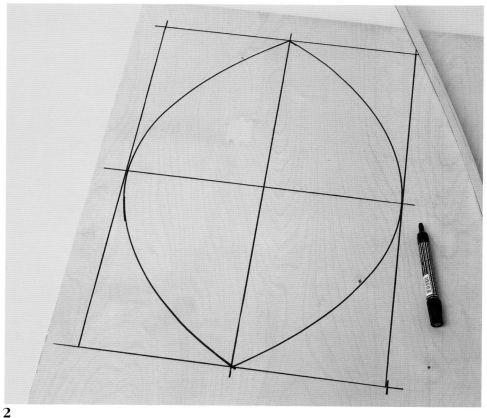

2

3

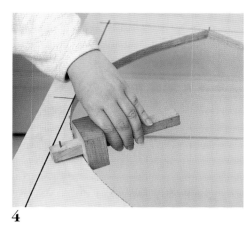

4

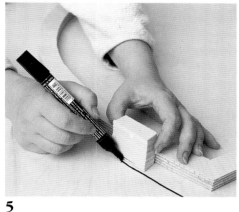

5

6

Step 4

Set the marking gauge to measure 1 in (2.5 cm) and score a line to mark the outer edge of the top rim. Cut this out carefully with the jigsaw. When you have done this, place on a clean part of the ¾ in (18 mm) ply and draw around it, inside and out, with a pencil and cut this out. You should now have two identical pieces.

Step 5

Using a small scrap of ply, roughly 1 in (2–3 cm) wide, draw around one of the pieces you have just cut out. Ask someone to hold it steady as you draw round it. Cut out the shape with the jigsaw. This will form the base.

Step 6

To make the feet, first cut out a rectangle of ply, in proportion to the base of the planter. Mark a square in pencil, draw the diagonal between two corners and follow this line to cut off a triangle. Use the wedge-shaped piece as a template for the other three feet, fitting them onto the piece cut from the center of the rim. Cut them out with a jigsaw.

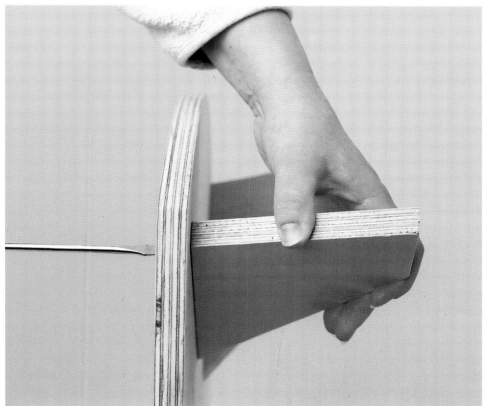

7

Step 7

Divide the solid base of the planter into four quarters. Use these pencil lines as a guide to drill two holes for each foot at equal distances from the edge. Drill two pilot holes in each foot on the longest sides of the wedges to correspond with the holes in the base. Glue and screw them together.

Using casters

An alternative to making feet would be to put casters on the base of the planter.

Day Two

Step 8
The underside of the base now has all its feet in position.

Step 9
Sand the edges on all the pieces to accentuate the lines of ply.

Step 10
Measure one side of the inside of the rim with a metal tape measure and add on a scant $\frac{1}{16}$ in because the sides have to fit snugly. Mark out two strips of $\frac{1}{16}$ in (1.5 mm) veneer, 10 in (25 cm) deep by the measurement you have just taken, remembering that the grain must run top to bottom, not side to side.

Step 11
Cut the veneer by scoring with a craft knife using the edge of a metal ruler as a guide.

Step 12
Fit the two strips into the inside of the two frames and trim to fit.

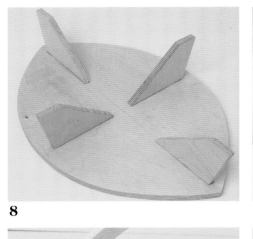

8

9

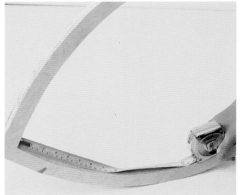

10

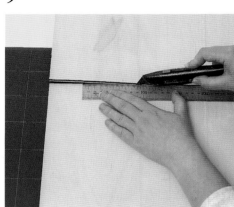

11

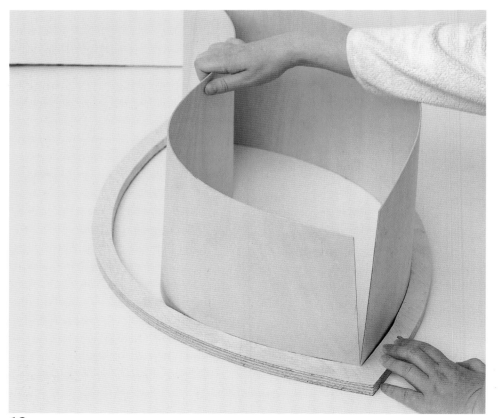

12

Using $\frac{1}{8}$ in (3 mm) veneer

If you are using $\frac{1}{8}$ in (3 mm) veneer as an alternative to $\frac{1}{16}$ in (1.5 mm), you will need to make sure your measurements are very accurate to ensure a good fit and prevent the need for trimming in position. You will probably need to cut a thicker veneer with a jigsaw rather than with a craft knife as has been done here.

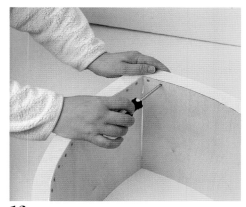

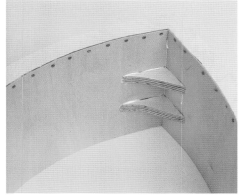

13

14

15

Step 13
Glue and screw the strips to the frames, top and bottom.

Step 14
Cut four blocks to support the inside from the middles of the frames; they should fit exactly. Screw and glue them to the inside.

Step 15
Put the completed top onto the base, so that it sits in the center. Draw a faint pencil line round the inside and outside. Drill holes through the base.

Step 16
Turn the whole planter upside down, match up the pencil lines to the sides and screw the base to the top. Paint on two coats of satin acrylic varnish to protect the surface.

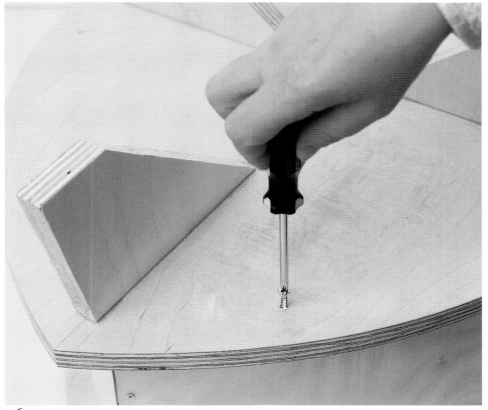

16

Recycled containers

This windowsill vegetable garden utilizes a number of containers that you would ordinarily throw away. They are transformed with paint and découpage.

Planning your time

DAY ONE
AM: Buy your materials; photocopy images

PM: Spray up tins and attach images

DAY TWO
AM: Cut up box and spray box and plastic container

PM: Plant all containers with chosen plant; put on windowsill

Tools and materials

Several containers, such as food storage bowls, tin cans, boxes

Enamel and/or acrylic spray paints

Access to a photocopier

PVA glue

Craft knife

Cutting mat

Butterfly tin opener

Spray varnish

Colored crayons or pencils

Pencil

These containers have all been made from disposable materials. They have served their purpose and are ready to be discarded, but rather than throwing them in the trash they can be recycled. On this windowsill there is a plastic food saver that has lost its lid, baked beans cans and a cardboard box.

All of them are sprayed using an enamel paint that is safe for children's toys and is suitable for containers that may hold foodstuffs. This paint is available from craft shops.

The plastic bowl food saver is sprayed with different layers of color; by allowing these to run you can create the effect of ceramic glaze. After painting the bowl can be sown with lettuce seeds.

The cans are sprayed with different colored enamels and decorated with colored-in photocopies of vegetables, taken from a book of copyright-free designs, to correspond with the vegetable growing in them. There are some designs you can use on page 76. You can also try decorating them with interesting food labels, or pictures cut from magazines.

The cardboard box has been cut down to make a plant tray, lined with a piece of plastic cut from a carrier bag, and sprayed with two colors that blend into each other.

This could be just the start of recycling and decorating your containers. No doubt you will have many other possible types of containers in your home that offer the potential for creative transformation.

1

2

3

Day One

Step 1

Start with the tin cans. Take the top off with a can opener that leaves the rim intact.

Step 2

Turn the can upside down, on a sheet of newspaper or wallpaper, and spray several coats of color on the tin, leaving it to dry between coats.

Step 3

Take photocopies of the decoration you want to put onto the can, enlarging or reducing to fit. There are some designs on page 76. Color it in as you wish. We used wax crayons, but you can use whatever type of paint or colored pencils you prefer to work with.

Step 4

Put the image on a cutting mat and cut it with a craft knife.

4

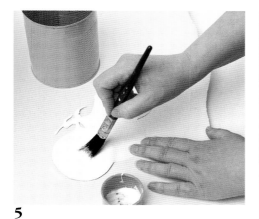

5

Step 5

Spread the back of the image with PVA glue and put in position on the can. When it has dried, seal the image with spray varnish.

Day Two

Step 6

To make the plant tray, mark the height of a plant pot against the base of a cardboard box.

Step 7

Draw a wavy line all around the base of the box.

6

Painting plastic

Enamel spray is perfect for covering plastic. Try using ice-cream containers, or cut up plastic drinks bottles to use as planters.

7

8

9

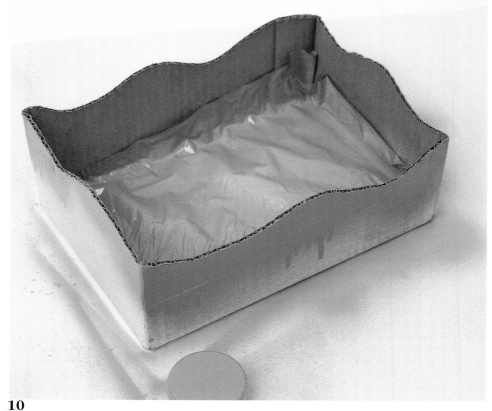

10

Step 8
Cut along the line with a craft knife.

Step 9
Cut up a plastic bag to line the base of the box and stick it down with PVA glue.

Step 10
Spray on a first coat of green enamel paint and leave to dry. Do not worry about any drips; they add to the character of the final effect.

Step 11
Spray on a second coat of contrasting color – orange is used here. Leave to dry before putting any pots with plants in the tray.

11

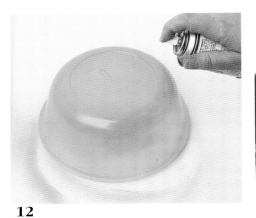

12

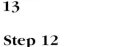

13

14

Step 12
Turn an old plastic bowl, the type for storing food in, upside down and spray it with orange enamel spray paint. Leave to dry.

Step 13
Spray a patchy second coat of blue on the bowl and leave to dry.

Step 14
Turn the bowl the right way up and stand on a plant pot. Spray a third color at close range and allow the paint to drip down the sides.

Step 15
Put gravel in the base for drainage, or alternatively punch holes in the bottom with a bradawl. Fill with potting soil and sow your chosen seeds or plants.

15

Templates

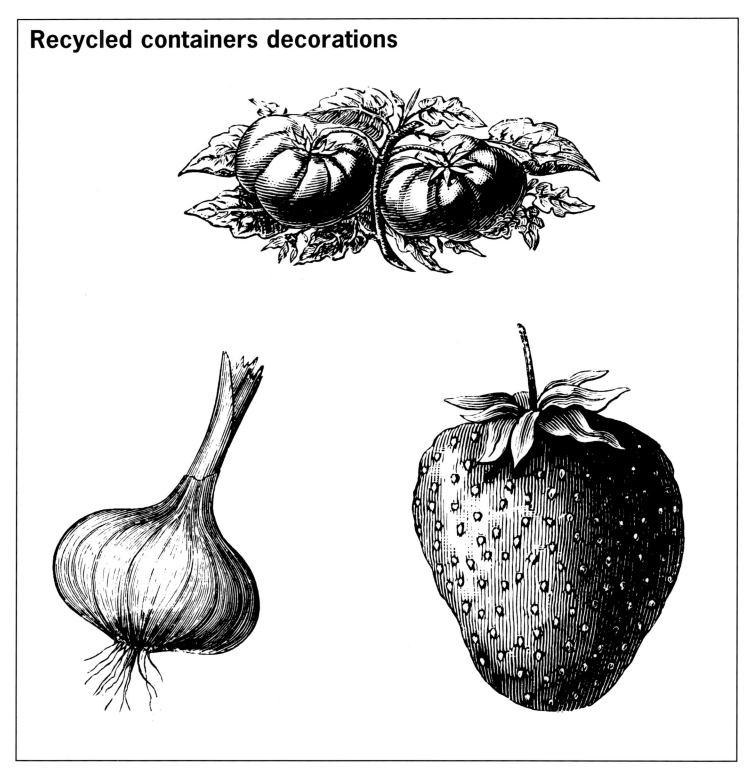

Recycled containers decorations

Painted tree template

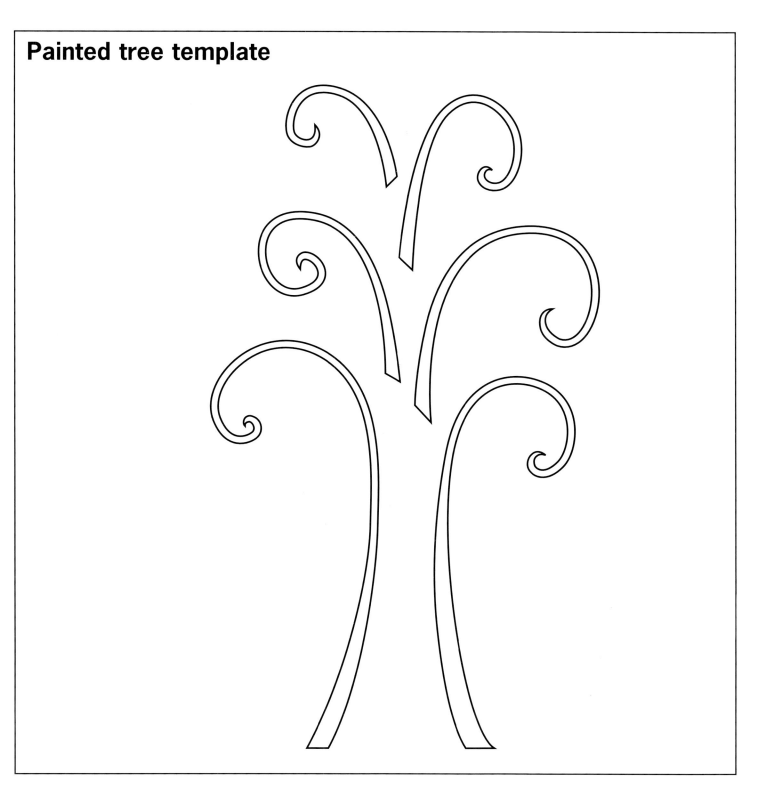

Glossary

Countersink bit

Flat wood drill bit

Marking gauge

Acrylic gold size
The glue used in gilding to apply metal leaf. Acrylic gold size is preferable because it dries more quickly than the oil-based equivalent.

Angle grind
A small circular saw for cutting brick, metal and other pipes. Use a masonry disk for cutting terracotta pipes.

Bradawl
A tool used to make a small hole in wood before fixing panel pins or screws – the starter hole helps prevent the wood from splitting.

Coach bolt
A long bolt with a flat end and rounded head to fit flush to whatever you are screwing to.

Copper Common nails
Copper nails with a big head, so they are easier to hit. Made of copper, they will not rust.

Countersink bit
An attachment for a drill that enlarges the top part of a previously drilled hole to allow the screw head to sit just below the level of the wood.

Finishing nails
Small steel or copper nails without a head so that they lie flush with the level of wood so that the tops are not visible.

Flat wood drill bit
A flat blade-like drill bit with a pointed end for drilling large holes in wood. The point makes a pilot hole for the flat blade.

Galvanized wire
Wire treated with zinc to make it rustproof.

Hacksaw
A small saw for cutting metal.

Hot melt glue gun
A gun with sticks of glue that melt when heated. It has a tendency to "string".

Jigsaw
An electric saw that allows you to cut intricate shapes. It has a base plate that can be angled for cutting. Different grades of blade give a different quality of cut.

Key
A key is a rough surface to which paint can adhere, prepared by rubbing down with sandpaper or wire wool.

Marking gauge
A tool that enables the user to mark lines accurately apart.

Medium density fiberboard (MDF)
Smooth board made of glue and compressed wood fibers. Particle board is a lower-quality alternative.

Metal leaf
Fine sheets of gilder's metal on a piece of backing paper.

Planed softwood
Pine or spruce wood that has had the bark removed and planed smooth in usable sizes. The sizes given in shops or lumber yards are unplaned sizes, just to confuse you.

Plywood

Thin veneers of wood bonded together in alternating layers so that the grain goes in different directions, giving strength and pliability. Usually made with wood with an attractive grain.

PVA glue (Polyvinyl acetate adhesive)

A white water-based glue that dries clear and gives a strong bond. EVA is the outdoor equivalent.

PVC pipe

Plastic pipe of differing diameters and length used for drainpipes.

Right angle

A junction of wood and metal set at a right angle, to ensure that joints are true right angles.

Sandpaper

Also known as glasspaper, sandpaper is available in various grades from very fine, for finishing work, to coarse grade or grit for heavier work.

Screw eyes

Screws with a loop on the end instead of a head, for hanging things from. Available in different sizes.

Size

The glue used in gilding to apply metal leaf.

Spray Varnish

Available in flat, satin, and gloss finish, spray varnish is easy to apply and dries quickly. Spray varnish is unsuitable on white paints because it can yellow with age.

Veneer

Thin slices of wood used to give an attractive face to an ordinary and inexpensive wood (such as plywood).

Vice

A vice will hold a piece of wood in place while you work on it. Usually a vice is screwed onto a workbench in a workshop, but portable workbenches, such as a Workmate, also have an integral vice.

Wall plugs

Enable you to screw into a wall or plasterboard where there is no natural grip for the thread of the screw. Wall plugs expand as the screw is turned. You should select the right size plug for the screws you are using.

Waterproof grout

Grout that is suitable for total immersion in water, such as in swimming pools. Most grout in DIY stores is not waterproof, so look for it in a builders' merchant.

Wood filler

Ideal for filling holes, buy ready-to-use filler in a tube or tub.

Wood stain

A wood stain allows the grain of the wood to show through and actually penetrates the surface to offer the wood protection against the elements.

Bradawl

Sandpaper

Wall plugs

Index